A TRUE BOOK™

The Hindenburg Disaster

PETER BENOIT

Children's Press®
An Imprint of Scholastic Inc.
New York Toronto London Auckland Sydney
Mexico City New Delhi Hong Kong
Danbury, Connecticut

Content Consultant
Tom D. Crouch, PhD
Historian and Museum Curator
Washington, DC

Library of Congress Cataloging-in-Publication Data

Benoit, Peter, 1955–
  The Hindenburg disaster/Peter Benoit.
      p. cm.—(A true book)
  Includes bibliographical references and index.
  ISBN-13: 978-0-531-20626-3 (lib. bdg.)   ISBN-13: 978-0531-28995-2 (pbk.)
  ISBN-10: 0-531-20626-2 (lib. bdg.)   ISBN-10: 0-531-28995-8 (pbk.)

  1. Hindenburg (Airship)—Juvenile literature. 2. Aircraft accidents—New Jersey—History—20th century—Juvenile literature. 3. Airships—History—Juvenile literature. 4. Airships—Germany—History—Juvenile literature. I. Title. II. Series.
  TL659.H5B46 2011
  363.12'4—dc22   2010045931

All rights reserved. Published in 2011 by Children's Press, an imprint of Scholastic Inc.
Printed in China. 62
SCHOLASTIC, CHILDREN'S PRESS, A TRUE BOOK and associated logos are trademarks and/or registered trademarks of Scholastic Inc.

5 6 7 8 9 10 R 18 17 16 15 14 13

Find the Truth!

Everything you are about to read is true *except* for one of the sentences on this page.

Which one is **TRUE**?

T or F The *Hindenburg* was able to float because it was filled with helium.

T or F Nobody knows the exact cause of the *Hindenburg* disaster.

Find the answers in this book.

Contents

THE **BIG** TRUTH!

Hindenburg's 1936 Transatlantic Flights

Zeppelin

The *Hindenburg*
taking off

4 The Final Flight

The *Hindenburg* crashes.

Newsreel services
filmed the crash
as it happened.

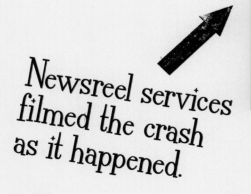

The *Hindenburg* in flight

CHAPTER 1

A Ball of Flame

On the evening of May 6, 1937, the German **airship** *Hindenburg* was landing at the Lakehurst Naval Air Station in New Jersey. The huge airship was completing its first flight of the year across the Atlantic Ocean. The airship floated close to the **mooring mast**. But suddenly, a burst of flame appeared. Within a minute, the entire craft was burning.

← If stood on end, the *Hindenburg* would have been taller than the Washington Monument.

A Fireball Crashing

The glorious airship was suddenly a fireball crashing down from above. The ground crew assisting the docking was terrified and started fleeing. Some members of the crew, however, stopped running and quickly raced back toward the *Hindenburg*. They knew it was their duty to help rescue anyone who survived.

Some lucky passengers escaped the burning ship and survived.

Workers help survivors of the *Hindenburg* explosion.

People on the ground run for their lives as the *Hindenburg* burns.

Filming the Disaster

In 1937, people did not have televisions at home. Everyone got their news from newspapers, radio, and **newsreels** that were shown in movie theaters. Five newsreel cameramen were at the airfield on May 6 to film the *Hindenburg*'s landing. They filmed the disaster from beginning to end.

The story of the *Hindenburg* disaster was on the front page of newspapers around the world.

"Oh, the Humanity!"

An announcer named Herbert Morrison was on the scene that day. He was describing the landing for radio listeners. By the end, he was sobbing:

It's practically standing still now. They've dropped ropes out of the nose of the ship. . . . It burst into flames! It burst into flames, and it's falling, it's crashing! Watch it! Get out of the way! . . . It's burning and bursting into flames, and the— and it's falling on the mooring mast

Reporter Herb Morrison (left) and sound engineer Charles Nehlsen with the record of the broadcast of the Hindenburg disaster

and . . . this is the worst of the worst catastrophes in the world. . . . Oh, the humanity! . . . I can't talk, ladies and gentlemen. . . . I'm gonna have to stop for a minute because I've lost my voice. This is the worst thing I've ever witnessed.

Morrison's eyewitness report can be heard on the Internet today.

An airship
demonstration
in 1905

CHAPTER 2

Airships

Airplanes first took flight in 1903, but it took many years before large, strong aircraft were built for long journeys. For decades before long-distance airplanes came along, there were airships. These gas-filled ships floated through the air. Passengers rode in a compartment on the bottom of the ship.

 Airships had been flying for more than 80 years before the *Hindenburg* took flight.

Rigid Airships

The *Hindenburg* was a **rigid airship**. These aircraft had a metal skeleton in an oval shape. This metal structure was covered with a cotton envelope. The ship floated because the envelope contained a number of fabric bags, or gas cells. They were filled with **hydrogen**, a gas that is lighter than air.

Rigid airships had **ballast** tanks filled with water, which added weight to the ship. The crew could drop ballast to climb or release some of the hydrogen to descend. During its flight, engines propelled the airship forward and allowed the crew to steer. When it was time to land, the crew released some of the hydrogen, which caused the ship to sink.

The *Hindenburg* was the largest aircraft ever built.

Building the *Hindenburg*

Early Airships

The *Hindenburg* was a **zeppelin**. Zeppelins were named for the German man who invented them: Count Ferdinand von Zeppelin. His first zeppelin flights took place in 1900. Soon, the count was offering sightseeing rides over German cities aboard his airships.

Count Ferdinand von Zeppelin

Eventually, Count von Zeppelin started a company called Luftschiffbau-Zeppelin to make the airships.

The first zeppelin was built in a work shed that floated on a lake so it could be turned to face the wind, which made launching the craft easier.

Germany used 115 airships during World War I. ➤

Zeppelins armed with guns on top were used to fire on enemy aircraft during World War I.

Airships at War

During World War I (1914–1918), Germany used zeppelins for several purposes. The ships could travel great distances with heavy loads, so they were used to spy on enemy armies and navies. During the war, Germany used zeppelins to drop bombs on London, England, and other enemy sites.

The *Graf Zeppelin*

After the war, the Zeppelin Company began building bigger and faster airships to travel greater distances. Some Zeppelins could reach a speed of 85 miles per hour (135 kilometers per hour). The *Graf Zeppelin* flew from 1928 to 1937, carrying passengers and goods everywhere. In 1929, it made a complete journey around the world. In 1931, it carried scientists on a special expedition to the Arctic.

In 9 years, the *Graf Zeppelin* traveled more than 1 million miles (1.6 million km).

The *Graf Zeppelin* under construction

People crowd around the *Graf Zeppelin* in Tokyo, Japan.

The *Hindenburg* being built in Germany in 1935

CHAPTER 3

The *Hindenburg's* History

Construction on the *Hindenburg* began in 1931. It would be the world's largest airship. It measured 804 feet (245 meters), which is longer than two and a half football fields. Five years later, it finally took flight on March 4, 1936. The *Hindenburg* carried 87 passengers on its first flight. Among them were 8 Zeppelin company airship captains, 47 other crew members, and 30 dockyard workers.

The *Hindenburg* was longer than three of today's Boeing 747 jets put end to end.

21

Large swastikas were painted on the *Hindenburg*'s tail fins.

A Symbol of Nazi Strength

In the mid-1930s, Germany was ruled by the Nazi Party. Because Germany had lost World War I, the Nazis wished to build Germany into the most powerful nation in the world. They saw the *Hindenburg* as a symbol of power. So the government often had the *Hindenburg* fly with the swastika showing. The swastika was the symbol of the Nazi Party. It is forbidden in modern Germany to display the swastika, the symbol of Nazi evil and brutality.

Flights Across the Atlantic

The *Hindenburg*'s main purpose was to carry passengers and goods across the Atlantic Ocean. These **transatlantic** flights would make a lot of money for Germany. The airship could carry up to 50 passengers from Germany to the United States in about 2.5 days. People were amazed by this. At that time, people normally traveled across the ocean by ship. The sea journey could take a week or longer.

A ground crew holds ropes to guide the *Hindenburg* on its takeoff.

Zeppelins had a ground crew of about 200 people.

First Atlantic Crossings

From March 31 to April 10, 1936, the *Hindenburg* first crossed the Atlantic Ocean on a trip to South America. It was a difficult trip, taking much longer than the planned 2.5 days. The engines failed twice, and the airship nearly crashed into the Sahara Desert in northern Africa. On May 6, 1936, after being repaired, the ship started its first regular flight from Germany to the Lakehurst Naval Air Station in New Jersey.

Going to and from Lakehurst, New Jersey, the *Hindenburg* often flew over New York City.

Because of the risk of fire, passengers could only smoke in a special smoking room.

Passengers on the *Hindenburg* relax in the dining room.

Traveling in Comfort

Passengers enjoyed comfort and convenience on *Hindenburg* flights. The passenger deck had 25 cabins with 2 beds in each. The beds were stacked as bunk beds. The rooms had sinks with running water, but passengers had to share a common bathroom. The deck also included a dining room, a writing and reading room, and lounges where people could gather.

Passengers spent most of their time in the common rooms, such as the main lounge.

The fabric walls of the lounge were decorated with a map of the world showing the routes of famous explorers.

Saving Weight

Because an airship had to float, it was important to keep as much weight as possible off the ship. The huge metal skeleton that formed the oval shape was made mostly of aluminum, a light metal. Furniture in the passenger compartment was made of aluminum. Sinks were made of plastic.

Fire Prevention

Hydrogen is dangerous if it is mixed with oxygen. One small spark touching this gas mixture can start a fire so hot that it cannot be put out. So any fire on board could be deadly, because it might cause the hydrogen gas cells to burst. The *Hindenburg* kitchen had an electric oven and stove, not a gas oven and stove. This was to guard against a gas flame causing a fire.

Cooks prepare a meal in the kitchen of the *Graf Zeppelin*.

27

First Air Journeys

Many airship passengers of the 1930s had never flown in any type of aircraft before. Even those who had flown were thrilled by a journey on the *Hindenburg*. The ship traveled smoothly and silently through the air. Large banks of windows gave people their first incredible views of Earth from above.

The *Hindenburg* often flew below the clouds, so passengers had great views from the windows.

Passengers watch as the *Hindenburg* lands in Lakehurst, New Jersey

The pilots in the control car of the *Hindenburg* usually kept the airship below the clouds.

Operating the Airship

When you fly in a plane today, two pilots sit at the controls in the cockpit. Controlling the *Hindenburg* was more like controlling a sea ship. A crew of at least 39 was needed to operate the airship. The captain and several crew members worked in a control car at the bow (front) of the ship.

Avoiding Bad Weather

It was important for the *Hindenburg* to avoid bad weather. Lightning and high winds could be deadly to the hydrogen-filled ship. So the captain watched the clouds carefully to anticipate storms ahead. He would sometimes fly many miles off course to avoid storms.

Timeline of Rigid Airship Travel

1900

The first zeppelin flight takes place.

1929

The *Graf Zeppelin* travels around the world.

Winter Break

After 17 successful transatlantic round-trip flights in 1936, the *Hindenburg* was taken out of service for the winter. Workers added 10 more cabins so that 72 passengers could be carried. They also added devices to collect rainwater for use as ballast. The *Hindenburg* returned to service in the spring of 1937.

1936

The *Hindenburg* makes its first flight.

1937

The *Hindenburg* crashes, and rigid airship travel ends.

Hindenburg's 1936 Transatlantic Flights

NORTH AMERICA

PACIFIC OCEAN

UNITED STATES

Lakehurst, New Jersey

ATLANTIC OCEAN

10 round-trips to Lakehurst, New Jersey, between May and October 1936

In the spring, summer, and fall of 1936, the *Hindenburg* completed 17 round-trip journeys across the Atlantic Ocean. Its two destinations were Lakehurst, New Jersey, and Rio de Janeiro, Brazil. More than 3,500 passengers and crew rode the *Hindenburg* across the ocean that year.

BRAZIL

PACIFIC OCEAN

SOUTH AMERICA

Rio de Janeiro

ATLANTIC OCEAN

7 round-trips to Rio de Janeiro, Brazil, between March and December 1936

The *Hindenburg* was docked at Lakehurst between flights in May 1936.

GERMANY
Frankfurt

EURO

AFRICA

The trip from Germany to Rio de Janeiro took 4 days.

N
W E
S

Airships were promoted as a romantic and luxurious way to cross the Atlantic.

CHAPTER 4

The Final Flight

In the early spring of 1937, the Zeppelin Company was looking forward to a second successful year of transatlantic travel. The *Hindenburg* made several flights within Europe and traveled round-trip to Brazil in March. It was scheduled to make 18 trips to New Jersey and back in 1937.

A one-way *Hindenburg* ticket cost $400. That would be more than $6,000 today.

Weather Delays

The *Hindenburg* left Germany on May 3, 1937. People in America waited with excitement for its first landing of the year. The Atlantic crossing went smoothly. But as the ship approached Lakehurst on May 6, Captain Max Pruss saw bad weather ahead. He turned the *Hindenburg* around and flew over the New Jersey coast to wait for the weather to clear. Almost 3 hours later, he headed back to Lakehurst.

The *Hindenburg* cruised at about 75 miles per hour (120 kph).

Americans on the East Coast looked to the sky on days when the *Hindenburg* was due to fly over.

The fire was ignited at the rear of the craft.

Fiery Disaster

At 7:21 p.m., Captain Pruss directed the *Hindenburg* toward the mooring tower at Lakehurst. His crew dropped landing ropes to the crew on the ground. And then disaster struck. Flames appeared at the rear of the ship at 7:25 p.m. The flames immediately mushroomed into a fire that rose above the ship.

Flames quickly consumed the *Hindenburg*.

In less than a minute, the entire ship had burned.

A Burning Heap of Metal

As the gas cells that held the *Hindenburg* afloat caught fire, the ship could no longer fly. The back end crashed first, and for a few moments the front end pointed toward the sky. A spurt of flame shot out from the top, and suddenly the entire ship was in flames. The front end then floated down, and the *Hindenburg* soon sat on the ground—a burning heap of metal.

62 Survivors

Because the ship was coming in for a landing, most of the passengers were standing at the observation windows. From there, they were able to escape the disaster. Those who were in their cabins or other interior rooms could not get out and died. Of the 36 people who died in the crash, 13 were passengers, 22 were the ship's crew, and 1 was a crewman on the ground. There were 62 survivors from the ship.

A passenger is carried away on a stretcher following the *Hindenburg* disaster.

What Caused the Explosion?

Historians and scientists have never agreed on the cause of the disaster. Some say that a mechanical failure punctured one of the hydrogen gas cells. Another explanation is that lightning struck the ship, but no witnesses saw lightning. Some even say that a person on board or on the ground caused the explosion intentionally.

The cause of the *Hindenburg* explosion is still not known.

A guard stands on duty beside the wreckage of the *Hindenburg*.

Modern Airships

Most people have seen today's airships, which are commonly called blimps. They are very different from the *Hindenburg*. They are **nonrigid airships**. They have no skeleton, just a huge balloon that fills with air. Blimps are filled with helium, not hydrogen. Helium is the same gas that is used to fill birthday balloons, and it is very safe. Unlike hydrogen, helium cannot burn.

Blimps often carry TV cameras that show sports events from above.

The End of an Era

The *Hindenburg* disaster brought an end to the era of rigid airship travel. But it was an era that was likely to end soon anyway. Even during the 1930s, airplanes were being built that could take passengers on long-distance flights. By the 1940s, transatlantic passenger flights had begun. By then, the *Hindenburg* was a tragic memory. ★

By the 1940s, it had become common for airplanes to fly across the Atlantic.

True Statistics

Hindenburg construction completed in: 1936

Length: 804 ft. (245 m)

Diameter: 135 ft. (41 m) at its widest part

Top speed: 85 mph (135 kph)

Length of flight from Germany to the United States: 60 hours

Number of transatlantic flights completed in 1936: 34 (17 round-trips)

Number of passengers and crew carried across the Atlantic: More than 3,500

Amount of mail and freight carried across the Atlantic: More than 66,000 lbs. (30,000 kg)

Did you find the truth?

(F) The *Hindenburg* was able to float because it was filled with helium.

(T) Nobody knows the exact cause of the *Hindenburg* disaster.

Resources

Books

Becklake, Sue. *100 Things You Should Know About Flight*. Broomall, PA: Mason Crest Publishers, 2009.

Doeden, Matt. *The Hindenburg Disaster*. Mankato, MN: Capstone Press, 2006.

Feigenbaum, Aaron. *The Hindenburg Disaster*. New York: Bearport, 2007.

Graham, Ian. *You Wouldn't Want to Be on the Hindenburg!* New York: Franklin Watts, 2009.

Majoor, Mireille. *Inside the Hindenburg*. Boston: Little, Brown, 2000.

Moore, Rob. *Why Do Airplanes Fly? All About Flight*. New York: PowerKids Press, 2010.

O'Brien, Patrick. *The Hindenburg*. New York: Henry Holt, 2000.

Organizations and Web Sites

Airships: The Hindenburg and Other Zeppelins

www.airships.net/hindenburg

Read a detailed history of the *Hindenburg* and other airships. See photos and movies of the *Hindenburg*, too.

Goodyear Blimp

www.goodyearblimp.com

Learn about the history of America's best-known fleet of nonrigid airships. See a slide show on how a blimp is built.

Hindenburg Disaster: Herb Morrison Reporting

www.otr.com/hindenburg.shtml

Hear the audio recording of radio announcer Herb Morrison's eyewitness account of the *Hindenburg* disaster.

Places to Visit

Lakehurst Naval Air Station

PO Box 328
Lakehurst, NJ 08733
(732) 818-7520
http://nlhs.com/nlhstours.htm

Visit the site of the *Hindenburg*'s many landings and takeoffs—as well as its final moments.

Smithsonian National Air and Space Museum

Independence Avenue at 6th Street SW
Washington, DC 20560
(202) 633-1000
www.nasm.si.edu

This immense museum includes a *Hindenburg* model and other artifacts.

Important Words

airship (AIR-ship)—a powered aircraft that is lifted into the air by gas that is lighter than air

ballast (BAL-uhst)—something that adds weight to a ship

hydrogen (HYE-druh-juhn)—a gas that is lighter than air and was used in some airships

mooring mast (MORE-ing MAST)—a structure attached to the ground to which a ship is tied

newsreels (NOOZ-reelz)—a short film that showed news events to people in movie theaters in the first half of the 1900s

nonrigid airships (NON-RIJ-id AIR-shipss)—airships that do not have a metal skeleton

rigid airship (RIJ-id AIR-ship)—an airship that has a metal skeleton

transatlantic (tran-suht-LAN-tik)—a journey that crosses the Atlantic Ocean

zeppelin (ZEH-puh-lin)—a type of airship with a hard frame and a soft envelope filled with gas cells

Index

Page numbers in **bold** indicate illustrations

About the Author

Peter Benoit is educated as a mathematician but has many other interests. He has taught and tutored high school and college students for many years, mostly in math and science. He also runs summer workshops for writers and students of literature. Mr. Benoit has also written more than 2,000 poems. His life has been one committed to learning. He lives in Greenwich, New York.